I AM

VANYALE THOMPSON

ISBN
978-1-958690-93-2 (Paperback)
978-1-958690-92-5 (Hardcover)
978-1-958690-94-9 (eBook)

Dedication

I dedicate this book to my family who taught
me that I should take God everywhere I go.

INTRODUCTION

My understanding of the bible.

There are all kinds of understandings that come from reading the bible. People usually judge by what they have heard or just take their own judgement from the readings. I, like most everyone else, was going by what I heard, until I sat down and read the bible myself.

As a child my mother used to take me and my siblings to church, the first thing I would do is get a piece of paper out and start to draw, not really listening, or maybe I really was listening. When I was older I read the bible for the first time myself and got my own understanding, or I'd like to say the understanding that the Lord gave me.

In this book I am trying to show what took place in the beginning from Adam to the time of Christ.

Vanyale Thompson

"In the beginning God created the heavens and the earth."

Gen 1

God calls on Light in Darkness. He separates the light from the darkness. He calls the light "Day" and darkness "Night."

Gen 1:3-5

God created two great lights and set them in the heavens. The greater light he called the "Sun" ruled over the day, and the lesser the "Moon" ruled the night.

Gen 1:16-18

God created many planets and set them in the heavens. There also were stars.

One of the planets he created was void
without form.

Gen 1:2

He separated the waters on the planet, and revealed dry land. He called the dry land "Earth," and the waters that were gathered together he called the "Seas."

Gen 1:3-5

On the earth a mist went up and watered
the whole face of the ground.

Gen 2:6

God said, "Let the earth produce vegetation, plants yielding seed, and fruit trees bearing fruit according to its kind."

Gen 1:11

In the waters, God created an abundance of
sea creatures according to their kinds.

Gen 1:20-21

God created every winged creature according to its kind that flew above the earth across the face of the sky.

Gen 1:20

God said, "Let the land produce living creatures according to their kinds: livestock, creatures that move along the ground, and wild animals."

Gen 1:24-25

God blessed them, saying "Be fruitful and multiply, and fill the waters in the seas, and let the birds multiply on the earth."

Gen 1:22

In God's image, according to his likeness
he formed a man from the dust of the ground,
and breathed into his nostrils the breath
of life; and man became a living being. The
man was named Adam.

Gen 1:26.2:7

He set Adam in a garden called Eden so that he could take care of it. In the midst of the garden there grew two great trees. One "The Tree of Life" the other "The Tree of Knowledge of good and evil."

Gen 2:15

Adam was told he could eat from every tree in the garden, but not from the tree of knowledge of good and evil. The day he eats from it he will die.

Gen 2:16-17

God brought all the animals to Adam so he
could give them names. He noticed all the
creatures had a mate but Adam had no helper.

Gen 2:20

God caused the man to fall into a deep sleep, and took one of his ribs. From the man's rib he created a woman, and brought her to the man.

Gen 2:22

Adam said, "She is bone of my bone and flesh of my flesh; she shall be called woman, because she was taken out of man." Adam named her Eve.

Gen 2:23. Gen 3:20

Adam and Eve lived in the garden naked
without shame.

Gen 2:25

God blessed them, and said to be fruitful
and multiply. He gave them dominion over
every living thing that moves on the earth.

Gen 1:28-30

They ate from all in the garden, except the tree of knowledge of good and evil.

The serpent was the most cunning creature
in the garden.

Gen 3:1

The serpent asked the woman, "Has God said, you shall not eat of every tree in the garden?"

The woman explained, "We could eat fruit from all trees, but the tree in the midst of the garden we can not touch, for if we do we will die."

Gen 3:2-3

The serpent said to the woman, "That you will not die."

The serpent would go on to tell her, "God knows that your eyes will be opened, and you will be like God knowing good and evil."

Gen 3:4-5

Eve desired the fruit from the tree of
knowledge, so she took one and ate.

Gen 3:6

She shared the fruit with Adam and they ate.

Gen 3:6

Adam and Eve's eyes were opened and they realized they were naked.

Gen 3:7

God called Adam and they hid. God asked, "Where are you?" Adam said, "I heard you in the garden, and I was afraid because I was naked."

Gen 3:10

God asked, "Who told you you were naked, have you eaten from the tree I forbid you?"

Adam said, "It was the woman you gave me, she gave me the fruit from the tree of knowledge, and I ate."

Gen 3:11

The woman said, "It was the serpent who deceived me, and I ate."

Gen 3:13

God said to the man, "Since you listened to the woman and ate from the tree which I commanded you not to eat, you shall be cursed."

Gen 3:17

God banished Adam out of the garden of Eden,
to till the ground that he was created from.

Gen 3:23

God set Cherubim, and a flaming sword
which turned every way, at the east of Eden
to guard the tree of life.

Gen 3:24

God cursed the serpent.

Gen 3:17-19

He cursed the woman.

Gen 3:16

God cursed the ground under man.

Gen 3:14-15

God said, "For dust you are, and to dust you will return."

Gen 3:19

Roman 5:19

19 For as by one man's disobedience many
were made sinners, so also by one man's
obedience many will be made righteous.

Roman 5:19

Corinthians 15:21-22

21 For since by man came death, by man also
came the resurrection of the dead.

22 For as in Adam all die, even so in Christ
shall all be made alive.

1 Corinthians 15:21-22

In the old testament of the bible many of the prophets preached the same message.

A Messiah would be sent to save his people from their sins. He would not come to destroy the Law or the Prophets, but to fulfill.

Isaiah 9:6. 7:14 . John 1:14-15. Matt 1:22-23. 5:17

This man would carry the weight of the world. God would send his only begotten son.

John 1:29

There would be a path set for him.

John 1:23

"The Lamb of God" would be sent from heaven.

John 1:29

He will come from the root and offspring of David.

Rev 22:16

He will be born to a virgin named Mary
in Jerusalem.

Luke 1:26-38

Mary's husband Joseph was puzzled by her pregnancy.

Matt 1:20-25

An angel appears to Joseph, and tells him
not to be angry, and that he should name the
child Jesus.

Matt 1:20

Shepherds from the east were given
knowledge of the child "Christ" by an angel,
and they followed a star to Jerusalem.

Matt 2:1-2

The shepherds visited Herod, the king in Judea, and they asked him about the child. Herod was troubled about the news of a new king.

Matt 2:3-12

The shepherds leave and find the baby Jesus born in a manger in a town called Bethlehem, and they shower the child with gifts.

Luke 2:12

Herod threatened the male children who were two years and under in Bethlehem. Joseph moves the family to Egypt, then later, he moves them back to the land of Israel.

Matt 3:13-16

Jesus grew to be strong in knowledge and the word of god.

Luke 2:52

Jesus was baptized by John, the baptist, in the river Jordan.

Matt 3:13

Jesus is tested in the wilderness. The
devil would say, "If you are the Son of God,
tell these stones to turn to bread."

Matt 4:3

He is tempted by the devil to jump from the pinnacle of the temple.

Matt 4:5

The devil told Jesus if he worships him he would give him the world. Jesus could not be tempted.

Matt 4:8-9

Jesus chooses twelve disciples.

Luke 6:12-16

Jesus had many women followers.

Mark 15:40

Many came to listen to Jesus preach the gospel and to see the miracles he performed.

Luke 5:1-11

Jesus fed the multitude with five loaves and two fish.

Matt 14:13-21

He walked on water.

Matt 14:22-33

Jesus calms storms by saying, "Peace be still."

Mark 4:39

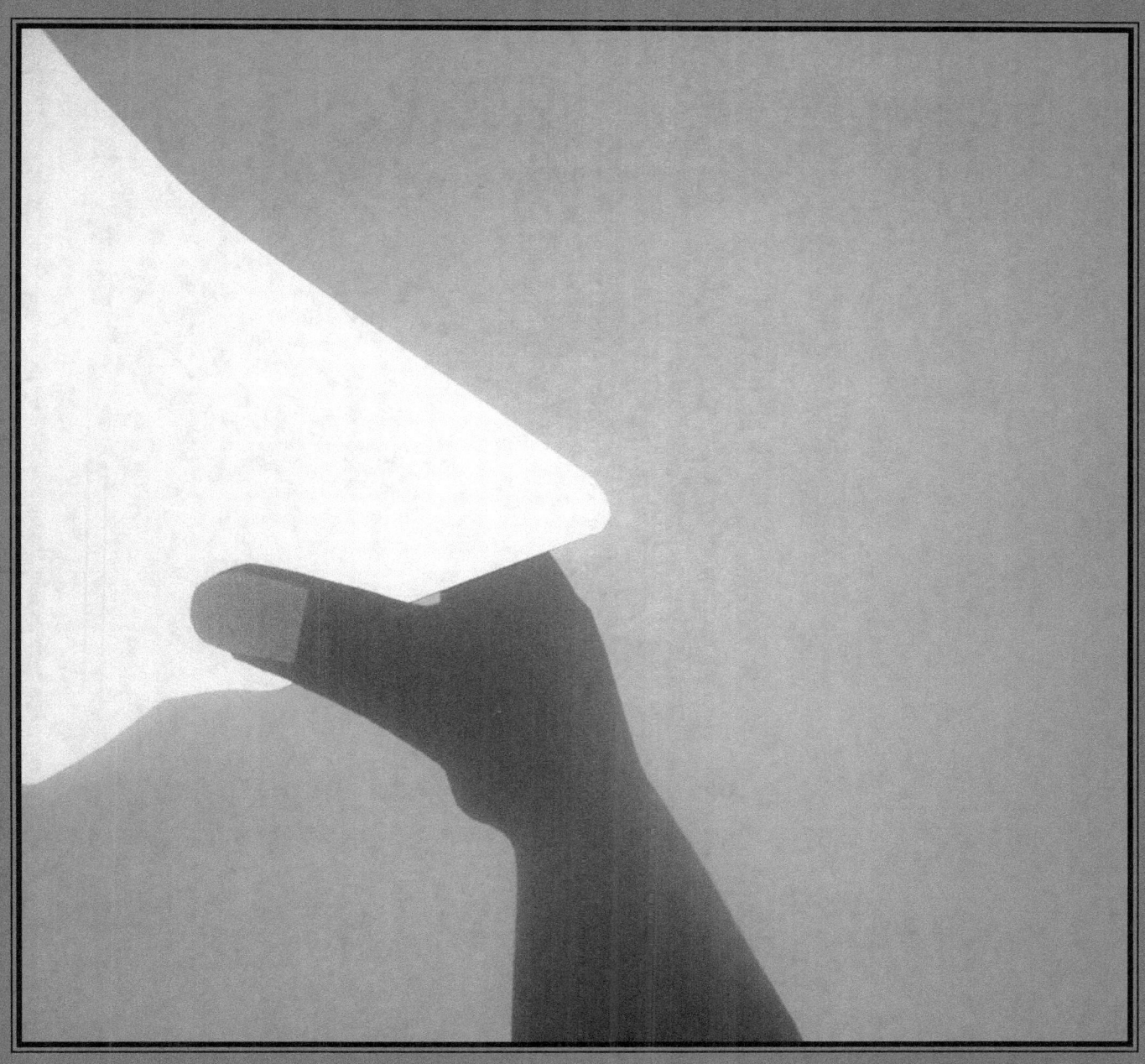

Just by touching the hem of his garment
people were healed. Jesus did many miracles.

Luke 8:43-48. John 21:25

Jesus taught with parables.

Matt 13:34

Men should pray always and not lose heart.

Luke 18:1

Jesus told his disciples to go out and teach, and if the people do not want to hear the Word, when they depart from that house or city, his disciples should shake the dust off their feet and walk on.

Matt 10:14

There were Pharisees, Scribes and Sadducees
who did not like Jesus's teaching. They thought
he was corrupting the people against god.

Matt 23:3-5

Jesus would say,

"I am the way and the truth and the life. No one comes to the Father except through me."

John 14:6

Jesus continued to preach the word of god in the cities of Israel.

Matt 11:1

Giving thanks, Jesus broke bread and said, "This is my body given for you; do this in remembrance of me."

Luke 22:19

He held up a cup of wine and said, "This is my blood which is poured out for the forgiveness of sins."

Matt 26:28

Not all of Jesus's disciples believed in
him. Judas Iscariot betrayed Jesus for thirty
pieces of silver.

Matt 26:1-25

Judas led the soldiers to Jesus. With a kiss he let them know who Jesus was.

Matt 26:47-49

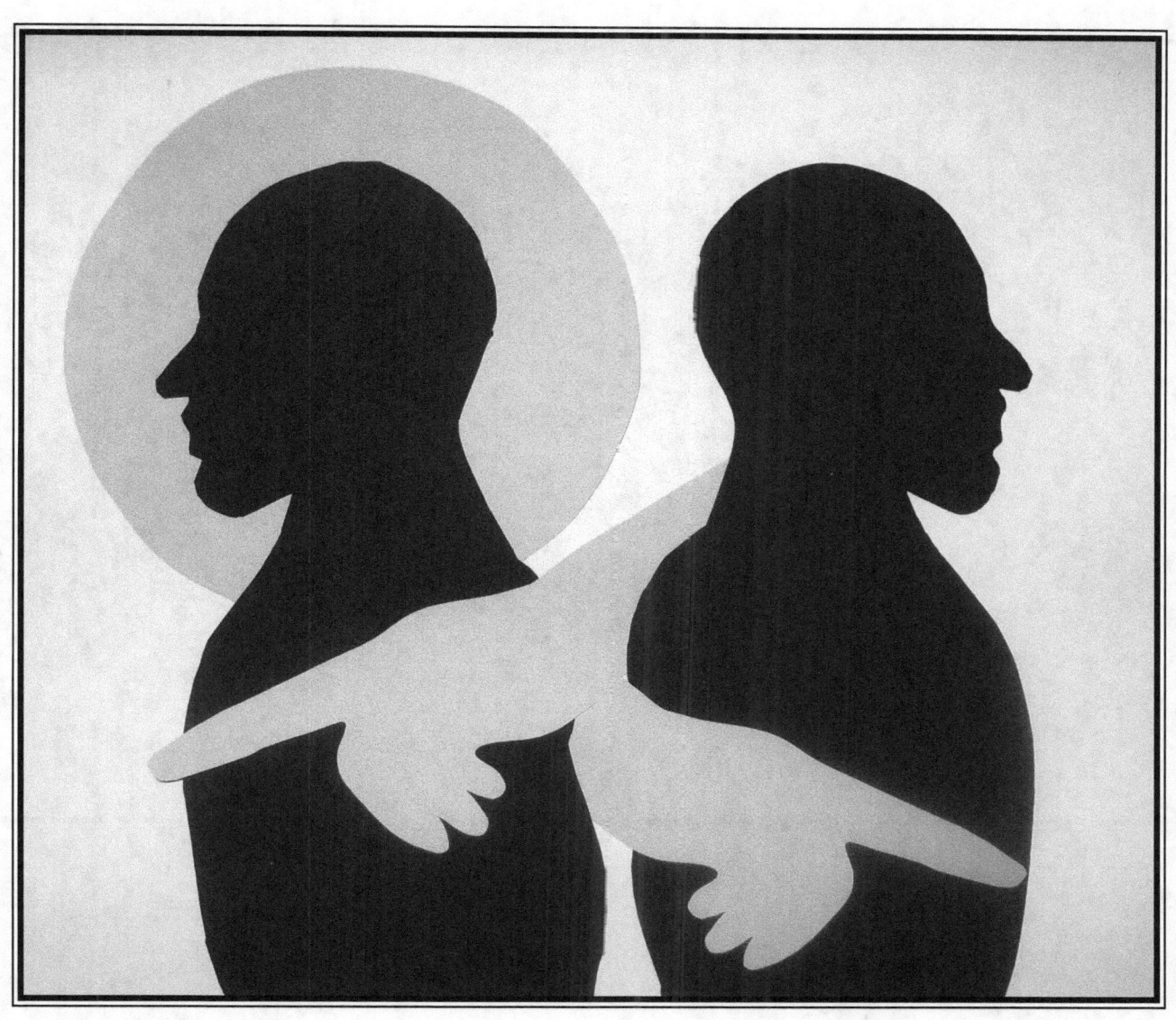

Jesus was taken in front of Pilate the governor, and the high priest, and the people to be judged.

Mark 15:1

The chief priest and council were seeking
false testimony against Jesus.

Matt 27:22-25

The people voted to crucify Jesus. Pilate took Jesus and had him scourged. There was a crown of thorns placed on his head and the people spit on him.

Mark 15:17-20, John 19:1-3

Jesus carries his cross to a place called,
"The Place of Skulls," where he was crucified.

John 19:17

"Jesus of Nazareth, King of the Jews," was written on a sign on his cross.

John 19:21

Jesus was buried in an unmarked tomb.

John 19:41

In three days Jesus will rise again; this
is the resurrection; you have to be of the
living to come back to life.

1 cor 15:4

After three days, Jesus rose back up on the earth, he appeared to his disciples and others.

Mark 16:14

Jesus taught his disciples to go into the world; preach the gospel to the people, and baptize in the name of Christ Jesus. If they believe, they will be saved.

Mark 16:15-16

Everything was fulfilled that had been spoken by the Prophets. Jesus ascends back to heaven.

Matt 1:22-23

Put your trust in
Jesus Christ the Lord.